MONSTER

Study Guide

Ana Verhar

Flying Pig Press

www.flyingpigpress.ch

Monster Study Guide
third revised edition September 2010
Ana Verhar

ISBN 978-3-033-02357-4

Cover and section titles font: *Bleeding Cowboys*, by Guillaume Seguin, www.lastsoundtrack.com. Used by permission.

Note: Page references in this study guide are based on the Harper Tempest paperback edition of *Monster* by Walter Dean Myers, with illustrations by Christopher Myers, ISBN 978-006-440731-4

We are all prisoners here,
Of our own device.

Eagles, *Hotel California*

If there are times when you are tempted to commit a crime, to go against what you know is
right to prove you're tough or cool, don't do it. And don't be fooled by people who may tell
you how much fun it is to be in prison. Just remember what I have told you, which is the truth
about what life in prison is really like – and stay out of here. Do not follow in my footsteps.

Stanley Tookie Williams, *Life in Prison*

S.T. Williams was the founder of the Crips gang,
on death row since 1981, executed on December 13, 2005.

Contents

Aims 6

Structure, Instructions, Assessment 7

Pre-Reading Tasks 8
    Choices 8
    Law and Order 1 10
    Punishment 11
    Crimes, Criminals, Criminal Actions 12
    Law and Order 2 13

Reading Sections Tasks 15
    Vocabulary Section 1 15
    Questions Section 1 16
    Writing Tasks 19

    Vocabulary Section 2 21
    Questions Section 2 22
    Writing Tasks 24

    Vocabulary Section 3 27
    Questions Section 3 28
    Writing Tasks 32

    Vocabulary Section 4 35
    Questions Section 4 36
    Writing Tasks 41

    Vocabulary Section 5 43
    Questions Section 5 44
    Writing Tasks 47

    Vocabulary Section 6 49
    Questions Section 6 50
    Writing Tasks 52

    Vocabulary Section 7 55
    Questions Section 7 56
    Final Writing Tasks 60

Analysis 64
    A: Fact and Non-Fact 64
    B: Witness Chart 65
    C: Guilty or Not Guilty? Reach a Verdict! 66
        C1: Steve Harmon 66
        C2: James King 67
        C3: Steve Harmon's Journal 68
        C4: Jury Deliberation Role Play 69

Questions for further consideration and discussion,
more ideas for writing tasks and role play activities 71

Text Type Composition Strategies 73
    Letter 73
    Letter 74
    Diary 75
    Newspaper Article 76

Final Factsheet 77

Aims

The primary aim of this study guide is for students to gain in-depth understanding of Walter Dean Myers' work *Monster*. Further aims are to engage students' curiosity, to provide a basis for discussion which motivates students to think critically about ethics, to develop students' awareness of literary devices and their effects and go beyond superficial understanding of mere plot and thus allow students to grow through their reading and critical reflection of literature. All activities in this study guide are designed to further students' writing, speaking, critical and analytical thinking skills, as well as their imagination and creativity. The wide range of activities and exercises offers teachers opportunities for varied assessment.

This study guide is divided into a pre-reading part introducing issues addressed in the work by asking students to make choices, express their opinion, and acquire some legal vocabulary; a main part structured into seven reading sections working closely with the text; an analysis part using graphic organizers to gain deeper insight into characters, interpersonal dynamics and ethics; a text type composition part to be used as a reference when completing the study guide's writing tasks. Many task formats are recurrent to help students know what to expect and experience progress, while some offer variation to fit the demands of the text or build up skills to complete progressively challenging assignments.

Teachers can assign the respective tasks in each section in their order of preference and / or use sections for different types of assessment. The study guide offers single-task assignments to be completed as a one-time event in class or as homework, but also tasks that can be worked on continuously. For instance graphic organizers such as the Fact and Non-Fact chart and the Witness Chart can be assigned either as a continuous task as the reading progresses, or as a summing-up-activity or even a test of students' analytical skills after the novel has been read.

The study guide is intended for grades 9-11 and can be used with native speakers or learners of English. Teachers of native speakers might choose to focus mainly on literary elements, the interpretation of select passages from the text, discussion of ethics, writing tasks and use comprehension questions and vocabulary exercises as a means to ensure that the work has been read. Teachers of learners of English on the other hand might focus on using particularly the main part of the study guide and vocabulary exercises to assist students in their reading of an unabridged literary text and boost their confidence by using the questions to let them experience how much they in fact understand without understanding every word. The study guide can also accommodate a layered curriculum if teachers choose to assign different tasks to different students and / or have students of different skill levels complete tasks jointly in cooperative learning activities. Aims, teaching methods, order of assigning tasks and sections in or out of class, expected or required quality of responses and assessment will naturally vary and be determined by the age and competence of the student as well as the school's curriculum policies.

MONSTER

Reading Sections:

Section 1: pages 1-13	**Due date:** a)_____ b)_____	**Test:** _____
Section 2: pages 14-46	**Due date:** a)_____ b)_____	**Test:** _____
Section 3: pages 47-99	**Due date:** a)_____ b)_____	**Test:** _____
Section 4: pages 100-148	**Due date:** a)_____ b)_____	**Test:** _____
Section 5: pages 149-205	**Due date:** a)_____ b)_____	**Test:** _____
Section 6: pages 206-237	**Due date:** a)_____ b)_____	**Test:** _____
Section 7: pages 238-281	**Due date:** a)_____ b)_____	**Test:** _____

For each section:

➢ **answer the questions in this study guide. Give clear references to the text.**

➢ **complete the vocabulary exercises for the section.**

➢ **complete the analysis parts (A, B, C) at the back of the guide.**

Unless otherwise instructed by your teacher, on <u>due date a)</u> you are required to have read the section, answered the questions, completed the vocabulary part. On <u>due date b)</u> you are required to have completed the analysis parts, and all other tasks assigned for that section. These tasks may include writing assignments, individual or group presentations, role play, research, or interpretation of specific passages.

<u>Tests</u> may include all or a selection of the following: writing tasks, multiple choice, true-false, mix and match, short answer questions, graphic organizers, gapped texts, contextualization and interpretation of passages, vocabulary exercises, etc. You are expected to know the events and characters of the text, the issues, background information, literary terms (and their application) discussed in class, the strategies and conventions of writing specific text types (such as diary, letter, speech, newspaper article, etc.). You are encouraged to use a dictionary and thesaurus for the completion of writing tasks.

<u>Assessment</u> includes all of the above possibilities. Your study guide entries will be graded, as will tests and tasks such as writing assignments, individual or group presentations, role play, in-class participation and depth of contribution. Be active in class, think deeply about what you read and how it is presented to you in the book, don't be minimalistic in your responses, and enjoy this monster!

Choices . . .

The questions below ask your opinion. Answer them by checking the box next to your preferred option, then briefly explain your choice in the space provided.

Would you rather... ?

1. ☐ not be able to tell time OR not know left from right? ☐

2. ☐ be an orphaned billionaire OR have a caring family and friends but little money? ☐

3. ☐ always speak in rhyme OR never hear every third word spoken to you? ☐

4. ☐ be in a relationship where you love your partner more OR less than s/he does you? ☐

5. ☐ go to prison because you are guilty OR go to prison because you were falsely accused? ☐

6. ☐ always lose OR never play? ☐

7. ☐ have all your teeth OR all your hair fall out? ☐

8. ☐ be transported backward OR forward to an unknown time and culture? ☐

9. ☐ be a girl OR a boy? ☐

10. ☐ be blind OR be paralyzed ☐ OR be deaf-mute? ☐

11. ☐ be the last-ranked person in an accelerated high school class OR

    the first-ranked person in a decelerated high school class? ☐

12. ☐ cheat on your partner OR be cheated on? ☐

13. ☐ commit a crime OR report a close friend to the police for committing a crime? ☐

14. ☐ have the ability to become invisible OR to fly? ☐

15. ☐ be unlucky in love OR never fall in love? ☐

16. ☐ be a character in your favorite movie OR be a real person? ☐

17. ☐ visit the Antarctic OR a sunny beach? ☐

18. ☐ not be able to count OR not be able to write? ☐

19. ☐ be sentenced to death and executed OR spend your entire life in prison? ☐

Law and Order 1

Match the offenses on the left with the definitions on the right by writing the correct number on the line.

1. Arson
2. Assault
3. Blackmail
4. Burglary
5. Embezzlement
6. Forgery
7. Fraud
8. Hijacking
9. Kidnapping
10. Libel
11. Manslaughter
12. Murder
13. Rape
14. Robbery
15. Shoplifting
16. Theft
17. Assassination
18. Bribery
19. Plagiarism
20. Drug trafficking
21. Hit and run
22. Looting
23. Mugging
24. Perjury
25. Pick-pocketing
26. Pilfering
27. Slander
28. Smuggling
29. Terrorism
30. Treason
31. Trespassing
32. Vandalism

____ taking a person away by force and keeping them prisoner, usually in order to demand ransom: money for their safe return.
____ stealing large amounts of money from a bank, a shop, or a vehicle, often using force or threats of violence.
____ copying things such as money bills, letters, official documents, signatures, etc. in order to deceive people
____ killing a person by accident or negligence
____ deliberately setting fire to a building
____ forcing someone to have sex
____ taking control of an airplane, train, bus, etc. by force, usually in order to make political demands.
____ demanding money or favors from someone by threatening to reveal a secret about them which, if made public, could cause the person embarrassment and harm.
____ deliberately taking goods from a shop without paying
____ stealing money that is placed in your care, often over a longer period of time.
____ getting money from someone by tricking or deceiving
____ printing or publishing something which is untrue and damages another person's reputation.
____ breaking into a house or apartment in order to steal things.
____ stealing
____ stealing things from people's pockets or handbags, usually in crowds or public places
____ saying something untrue about someone with the intention of damaging his or her reputation.
____ deliberately damaging public or private property, usually just for the fun of it.
____ offering money or gifts to someone in a position of authority in order to persuade them to help you
____ lying in court while giving testimony when you have sworn to tell the truth.
____ taking things or people illegally into or out of a country
____ murdering a public figure or important person such as a king or president
____ entering privately owned land or property without the permission of the owner
____ attacking someone, usually in a public place such as a dark alley in order to rob him or her.
____ trading in illegal drugs, such as heroin, marihuana, etc.
____ betraying your own country by helping its enemies
____ stealing small amounts of goods or things of little value, often over a long period of time
____ a car accident in which the guilty driver does not stop to help
____ the use of violence such as murder and bombing in order to obtain political demands or influence a government.
____ stealing from shops, buildings, homes, etc. left unprotected after a violent event or natural desaster such as a war, terrorist attack, or earthquake.
____ copying another person's ideas or writings and presenting them as your own
____ the intentional unlawful killing of someone
____ an attack, usually including physical injury

Punishment

Explain the common expression: "The punishment should fit the crime."

The Babylonian king **Hammurabi** is best remembered for his code of laws written around 1700 BC. Here is an extract from it:

> If a man brings an accusation against a man, and charges him with a crime, but cannot prove it, he, the accuser, shall be put to death.
> If a builder builds a house for a man and does not make its construction firm, and the house which he has built collapses and causes the death of the owner of the house, that builder shall be put to death.

What do you find striking about Hammurabi's law code? What might be advantages or disadvantages of this law code? Do you find that the proposed punishments fit the crimes?

Singapore has very strict laws regarding cleanliness and public or private property. The common punishment for vandalism, for example, is to be hit with a cane – a four-foot-long, half-inch-wide piece of wood or bamboo – one or many times depending on the crime.

In 1994, American teenager, Michael Fay, was accused of spray-painting parked cars and had in his possession street signs he had stolen. When brought to trial, Michael Fay admitted that he had committed the crimes, and he awaited to hear the punishment. What do you think the punishment was? How do you think Americans reacted when hearing the story reported by the media?

Look at the offenses below. **Rate** them according to which you find the most serious and the least serious, by numbering them 1 (least serious) to 21 (most serious). Justify your rating.

    a) arson
    b) disrespecting your parents
    c) cheating in school
    d) littering
    e) shoplifting or theft
    f) armed robbery
    g) murder
    h) euthanasia
    i) using drugs
    j) vandalism
    k) telling a lie
    l) rape
    m) forging a signature
    n) speeding
    o) torturing an animal
    p) skipping class
    q) plagiarism
    r) assault
    s) hit and run
    t) cheating on your significant other
    u) dealing drugs

What punishments fit the above offenses? Justify your answers.

Crimes, Criminals, Criminal Actions

Noun (offense)	Noun (person)	Verb	Related words
arson			
assault			
blackmail			
burglary			
	conspirator		
embezzlement			
forgery			
fraud			
kidnapping			
murder			
rape			
robbery			
shoplifting			
theft			
assassination			
mugging			
perjury			
smuggling			
terrorism			
treason			
vandalism			

Law and Order 2

Complete the sentences with the correct words from the box. Use the correct verb form!

arrest	culprit	try	charge	court	detain
evidence	sentence	plead	oath	parole	cell
fine	fingerprints	find	handcuff	investigate	judge
clues	testimonies		theft	witnesses	

A policeman was sent to _____ the disappearance of some property from a hotel. When he arrived, he found that the hotel staff had caught a boy in one of the rooms with a camera and some cash. Several other _____ led the policeman to believe that the boy was the _____: his hat was found in the hotel-room, and the credit card he carried did not have his name on it. When the policeman tried to _____ the boy, he became violent and the policeman had to _____ him. At the police station the boy could not give a satisfactory explanation for his actions and the police decided to _____ him with the _____ of the camera and cash. They took his _____, locked him in a _____, and _____ him overnight. The next morning he appeared in _____ before the _____ to be _____. He took an _____ and _____ not guilty. Two _____, the owner of the property and a member of the hotel staff, gave _____. The Crime Scene Unit presented _____. After both sides of the case had been heard the boy was _____ guilty. He had to pay a _____ of 1500$ and he was _____ to three months in prison suspended on a 2-year _____.

Put the correct preposition from the box in each space.

before	in	to	of	under	with

He's being kept _____ custody.

He was sentenced _____ five years without parole.

She got a sentence _____ six months.

You are _____ arrest. You have the right to remain silent. Everything you say…

He was accused _____ murder.

She's been charged _____ manslaughter.

He appeared _____ court _____ handcuffs.

They were brought _____ the judge.

The jury reached a verdict _____ guilty.

He lied _____ oath.

The murderer has to go _____ prison.

Tookie Williams spent 10 years _____ prison.

Complete the sentences with the correct words from the box. Use the correct verb form!

attorney	autopsy	bail	barrister	coroner	death penalty
defense attorney	defendant	gavel	jury	alibi
plaintiff	prosecutor	trial	verdict	victim
abolish	accomplice	sue	convict	prove
interrogate	warrant	threaten	lawyer	acquit

If you need legal advice in Britain or America you go to a _____. If you need legal representation in court, you go to the _____ in Britain or the _____ in America. The lawyer representing the person charged with a crime is the _____. His client is the _____. The lawyer working for the state and accusing a person of a crime is the _____. The person against whom a crime has been committed is the _____. The person accusing someone of a crime against him or her is the _____. That person _____ the suspected criminal.

Before someone can be _____ of a crime, the accuser has to _____ that person's guilt beyond a reasonable doubt. To do this, the police will _____ the suspect and other people to find out whether someone is lying. They will also try to get a _____ that gives them the right to search the suspect's house, computer, or get his phone records. They will further check if the _____ is true that the suspect's friend has provided that claims the suspect was in a different place at the time the crime was committed. Sometimes a criminal has had a helper or assistant, his _____, and the police will try to find that person too. The police will also try to find out whether that person was _____ by the suspect or whether he helped voluntarily.

Sometimes a criminal can be free until the date of his trial if he pays a certain amount of money as security. That is called to make _____. If a person dies in suspicious circumstances, an _____ is done by the _____ to find out the cause, time, and manner of death. This can also help ascertain someone's guilt.

At the end of a _____, the judge orders the twelve men and women of the _____ to retire and consider their _____: guilty or not guilty. If these people find a person not guilty, he is _____ and let go. In some countries murderers are executed, but other countries have _____or given up the _____.

The little hammer the judge uses to install order in the courtroom is called a _____.

Vocabulary Section 1 (pages 1-13)

All of the words below are from this reading section. They are listed in order of their appearance in the text. Verbs are given in the infinitive. Match the words with the correct definition by writing the correct number on the line.

1. scream	___ someone who has seen a crime and testifies in court
2. scratch	___ not clear or smooth, but with a rough pattern
3. rectangle	___ proceedings in court to determine culpability
4. recognize	___ a person you do not know
5. trial	___ a formal proposal to do something
6. guard	___ confirm, admit, take notice of something
7. rubber	___ cause pain or injury, harm someone
8. get used to	___ geometric shape with four right angles
9. grainy	___ identify
10. hurt	___ offensive, indecent
11. scene	___ someone who protects you or makes sure you do not escape
12. experience	___ very stern, disagreeable
13. grim	___ making a loud sound with your voice, for help, out of pain or anger
14. inmate	___ where a film is projected onto
15. yell	___ continuous action between two cuts in a film
16. obscene	___ speak very loudly or angrily
17. cot	___ the action you take if something itches
18. sink	___ back part of something
19. court	___ violent person or criminal
20. the john	___ small, benchlike place where you sleep
21. blanket	___ person in a prison
22. opening credits	___ tough, elastic substance
23. blur	___ the toilet
24. screen	___ when you are not sure about something, disbelief
25. bars	___ people who give a guilty or not guilty verdict in court
26. prosecutor	___ something you cover yourself with in bed
27. doubt	___ place where a trial is held
28. thug	___ lawyer that works for the state and against suspected criminals
29. handcuff	___ when something becomes familiar or normal
30. witness	___ what you learn from an action or event
31. stranger	___ capital punishment, punish by taking someone's life
32. rear	___ iron-chain used to bind someone's hands
33. motion	___ information on the creators and participants of a film
34. death penalty	___ something unexpected
35. jury	___ a water basin with taps and a drainage pipe
36. acknowledge	___ iron or other solid-material that forms a barrier
37. surprise	___ make indistinct, impossible to perceive clearly

Questions Section 1   (pages 1-13)

1. Where is the narrator? Find words in the text that suggest his whereabouts.

_____

_____

_____

2. Which three scenes from this place does he describe?

_____

_____

_____

_____

3. What does the narrator mean by "if your life outside was real"(3)?

_____

_____

_____

4. What is the narrator's main impression of this place?

_____

_____

_____

5. How does the narrator intend to "survive" or "get used to" this place?

_____

_____

_____

6. Why does the font and layout change on page 7?

_____

_____

_____

7. What is the purpose of the use of different fonts?

_____

_____

_____

8. What is the setting of the "movie"?

_____

_____

_____

9. What is the title of the "movie"? How might it influence the opinion of the viewer?

_____

_____

_____

_____

_____

10. Who is the narrator and what do we know about him?

_____

_____

_____

_____

11. Which other characters appear? What is their occupation? How are they characterized?

_____

_____

_____

_____

_____

_____

12. What does the narrator mean by suggesting that Kathy is "all business" (12) ?

_____

_____

_____

13. Is the narrator reliable? Justify your answer.

_____

_____

_____

_____

_____

_____

14. Analyze the passage below. Who speaks it? What is striking about it? What atmosphere is created through this passage? How might the passage connect to the entire work?

I have seen movies of prisons but never one like this. This is not a movie about bars and locked doors. It is about being alone when you are not really alone and about being scared all the time. (4)

_____

_____

_____

_____

_____

_____

_____

_____

_____

_____

_____

_____

_____

Writing Tasks

Write at least 150 words.

1. Have you ever felt like your life was a movie? If yes, why? How was it different from "reality"? How is a movie different from reality in general?

2. Have you ever been accused of something that you did wrong? What was it? How did that make you feel? How did you get out of it? How were you punished? Was this punishment effective – why yes, or why not? Would you or did you do this "wrong deed" again?

3. "There is no truth, there is no true fact". Do you agree or disagree with this statement? Justify your answer. If you agree, how can we then determine who is guilty and who is not?

4. "Everybody lies". Do you agree or disagree with this statement? Justify your answer. If you agree, how can we then determine who is guilty and who is not?

5. Would you rather be a prosecutor or a defense attorney? Explain your answer.

_____
_____
_____
_____
_____
_____
_____
_____
_____
_____
_____
_____
_____
_____
_____
_____
_____
_____

Vocabulary Section 2   (pages 14-46)

All of the words below are from this reading section. They are listed in order of their appearance in the text. Verbs are given in the infinitive. Match the words with the correct definition by writing the correct number on the line.

1. shackle	___ attack, worry, or annoy repeatedly
2. unshackle	___ speak or act on behalf of someone, stand for something
3. evident	___ not exactly, about, more or less
4. suppress	___ witness statement in court
5. testimony	___ the machine used to process payments in a shop
6. intense	___ main attorney presenting in a trial
7. lead counsel	___ hinder, stop, obstruct, slow down
8. admissible	___ an active member of something
9. casual	___ obvious, clearly apparent
10. predictable	___ advantage, profit
11. viewer	___ iron chains used to bind someone's feet
12. represent	___ someone who watches a movie
13. threaten	___ something that can be admitted, fits the rules
14. participant	___ the breaking of a rule
15. merit	___ point out, make stand out, give importance
16. infringe	___ chance
17. disregard	___ informal, relaxed
18. approximately	___ release someone from locked chains
19. defend	___ someone who helps another commit a crime
20. evidence	___ what you own
21. conspiracy	___ disrespect, not caring about something
22. impede	___ worthiness, whether something deserves praise or has quality
23. commit	___ extreme, fierce, strong
24. charge	___ mistaken, imperfect, wrong
25. intent	___ use in a specific situation
26. apply	___ keep from being known or used, hide, withhold
27. flawed	___ you can tell what will happen next
28. overwhelm	___ calculating for one's own good
29. self-serving	___ protect something or someone
30. emphasize	___ state intention to harm or hurt someone in order to get something
31. accomplice	___ accuse someone formally of something
32. opportunity	___ when something is too much for you
33. cash register	___ carry out something (usually a crime)
34. property	___ proof
35. harass	___ attentive, focussed, with concentration
36. benefit	___ when more than one person is involved in a plan to do something criminal
37. oppress	___ govern harshly, tyrannize

Questions Section 2   (pages 14-46)

1. Why might the narrator suggest that the judge looks bored (17) ?

_____

_____

_____

2. Who is Mr. Sawicki?

_____

_____

3. What does Mr. Sawicki feel is the most important feature of a film? Do you agree?

_____

_____

_____

_____

4. What is the narrator accused of?

_____

_____

5. What does the fact that Steve writes "monster" all over his pad show about him?

_____

_____

6. What purpose does the flashback to a scene from Steve's life four years ago serve?

_____

_____

_____

_____

7. Begin completing the witness chart on page 65 in the analysis part.

8. Analyze the passages below. Who speaks them? What is striking about them? What is suggested or meant by them? Why are they included at this point in the work, what is their purpose? How might the passage connect to the entire work? Do you agree with the statements made in the passages?

   a. My job is to make sure the law works for you as well as against you, and to make you a human being in the eyes of the jury. (16)

   b. But there are also monsters in our communities – people who are willing to steal and to kill, people who disregard the rights of others. (21)

   c. But if I didn't think of the movie I would go crazy. (45)

_____

_____

_____

_____

_____

_____

_____

_____

_____

_____

_____

_____

_____

_____

_____

_____

_____

_____

_____

_____

_____

_____

Writing Tasks

Write at least 150 words.

1. Do you like or dislike Steve? Explain your answer.

2. Do you think it is fair that Steve is charged for the same crime as King?

3. Review the opening of the trial from Steve's mother's perspective as she might write it in her diary.

4. Review the opening of the trial at the Harmon's dinner table by noting the conversation between father, mother and Jerry in dramatic style.

_____

_____

_____

_____

_____

_____

_____

_____

_____

_____

_____

_____

_____

_____

_____

_____

_____

_____

_____

_____

_____

_____

_____

Vocabulary Section 3   (pages 47-99)

All of the words below are from this reading section. They are listed in order of their appearance in the text. Verbs are given in the infinitive. Match the words with the correct definition by writing the correct number on the line.

1. intent to distribute	___ when an attorney questions a witness of the opposing party
2. drop charges	___ using the device that makes a firearm shoot
3. a getover	___ a person who was hurt or damaged
4. cop (as used on p 51)	___ row between chairs, desks, people, houses, shelves
5. harmful	___ immediate, one moment
6. harm	___ stop accusing formally of a crime
7. assault	___ the one who checks whether the coast is clear
8. adjourn	___ swell or puff up with gas or liquid
9. reconvene	___ (verb) speak or turn against something, refute
10. lookout	___ (noun) flat-topped structure over which goods are sold to customers
11. curse	___ hurtful, dangerous
12. appeal	___ official term for dealing drugs
13. bloated	___ competition
14. delay	___ violent physical attack
15. aisle	___ short
16. pale	___ sicklish, white-colored
17. counter	___ a robbery
18. stoop	___ the person we assume has committed a crime
19. increase	___ show, point out
20. decrease	___ hunched over, not standing completely upright
21. victim	___ break off a meeting until later
22. suspect	___ where you are locked up and wait to be executed if you have been sentenced to death
23. pull the trigger	___ set up, make permanent, prove
24. lethal injection	___ everything that pertains to the legal proceedings of a party
25. death row	___ steal
26. cross-examine	___ become larger in size or amount
27. establish	___ come back together for a meeting
28. perpetrator	___ the person who committed the crime, culprit
29. case	___ hurt
30. contest	___ use swearwords
31. indicate	___ syringe filled with poison used in executions
32. brief	___ become smaller in size or amount
33. instant	___ attempting a new trial after a conviction
	___ postpone, when something does not start when scheduled

Questions Section 3   (pages 47-99)

1. What purpose does the cut on page 57 to the prison cell serve?

_____

_____

_____

_____

_____

_____

2. Which superhero would Steve like to be and why? What does this show about his personality?

_____

_____

_____

_____

_____

_____

3. When is the only time Steve feels involved or part of the case?

_____

_____

4. What is the worst about prison for Steve?

_____

_____

_____

5. How does O'Brien think the case is going? Do you agree with her assessment?

_____

_____

_____

6. What do we learn in the flashback on pages 80-82?

_____

_____

_____

_____

_____

_____

_____

7. What does Osvaldo's testimony show? (recommend: compare it to the flashback!)

_____

_____

_____

_____

_____

8. Why do you think Steve includes the junior high school students in his notes? Write down what the teacher says to them and how the students react to Steve.

_____

_____

_____

_____

_____

_____

_____

_____

_____

_____

_____

_____

_____

9. Analyze the passages below. Who speaks them? What is striking about them? What is
    suggested or meant by them? Why are they included at this point in the work, what is their
    purpose? How might the passages connect to the entire work? Do you agree with the
    statements made in the passages?

    a. I like the last scene in the movie, the one between me and Jerry. It makes me seem like a real
        person. (60)

    b. In a way he was right, at least about me. I want to look like a good person. I want to feel like
        I'm a good person because I believe I am. (62)

    c. I couldn't sleep most of the night after the dream. The dream took place in the courtroom. I
        was trying to ask questions and nobody could hear me. I was shouting and shouting but
        everyone went about their business as if I wasn't there. (63)

    d. Older Prisoner: They got to give you some time. A guy dies and you get time. That's the deal.
        Why the hell should you walk? And don't give me young. Young don't count when a guy dies.
        Why should you walk?
        Steve: 'Cause I'm a human being. I want a life too! What's wrong with that?
        Older Prisoner: Nothing. But there's rules you got to follow. You do the crime, you do
        the time. You act like garbage, they treat you like garbage. (76)

    e. How's he gonna say he's innocent? That's why they holding the trial – so the jury can say if
        he's innocent or not. What he says now don't even count. (77)

    f. You ain't got the heart to be nothing but a lame. Everybody knows that. You might be
        hanging out with some people, but when the deal goes down, you won't be around. (82)

    g. "All they can do is put me in jail", he said. "They can't touch my soul." (89)

    h. I think about myself so much, about what's going to happen to me and all, that I don't think
        about my folks that much. I know she loves me, but I wonder what she's thinking. (91)

    i. They do things to you in jail. You can't scare somebody with a look in here. (97)

_____

_____

_____

_____

_____

_____

_____

_____

_____

Writing Tasks

Write at least 200 words.

1. If you could be a superhero, who would you be? Justify your answer.

2. If Steve were found guilty, how do you think he might feel about the death penalty? Use passages from the text to back up your claims.

3. Should we have the death penalty or not? Explain your answer.

4. Should 16-year old Steve be tried as an adult? Justify your answer.

5. Write a diary entry from Steve's perspective about what he misses from the outside world. What would he think about? Would he regret anything?

_____
_____
_____
_____
_____
_____
_____
_____
_____
_____
_____
_____
_____
_____
_____
_____
_____
_____
_____
_____
_____
_____

Vocabulary Section 4   (pages 100-148)

All of the words below are from this reading section. They are listed in order of their appearance in the text. Verbs are given in the infinitive. Match the words with the correct definition by writing the correct number on the line.

1. treat	___ divine assistance or forgiveness
2. apprehend	___ go across
3. oath	___ cry
4. struggle	___ cruel, wild, violent
5. disposable	___ without hope
6. diapers	___ whisper, speak without making loud sounds
7. reassure	___ trick, deceive
8. weep	___ how you behave towards someone
9. sob	___ defense
10. drugstore	___ sound you make when vomiting
11. cacophony	___ being undisturbed and unobserved
12. within earshot	___ when you die because your lungs fill with water
13. crowd	___ decision of the jury
14. angle	___ something urgent
15. distinguish	___ sound you make when crying
16. resident	___ publicly inform
17. peek	___ give, reserve for
18. rush	___ find
19. demand	___ unharmonious mixing of sounds
20. vicious	___ under
21. dismay	___ place where you can buy toiletries and medicine
22. culprit	___ being saved from disaster or sin
23. announce	___ twist, pull hard or violently
24. determined	___ can be thrown away
25. deserve	___ feeling of shock
26. protection	___ move very fast (fits 2 words!)
27. hustle	___ have difficulty with, fight with
28. desperate	___ catch, arrest
29. blank	___ inhabitant, someone who lives in a specific place
30. gag	___ loud
31. merchandise	___ confuse
32. emergency	___ empty
33. perimeter	___ tell apart, see a difference
34. beneath	___ being sure of something
35. mention	___ a certain perspective or point of view
36. bullet	___ the use of excessive physical force
37. traverse	___ have fun, be happy, celebrate
38. recover	___ extent of something, outer edge or boundary
39. certainty	___ ask for, command
40. drown	___ what babies wear instead of underwear
41. tilt	___ when you feel for someone
42. embarrassed	___ the small metal piece that shoots out of a firearm
43. tighten	___ swear, make a formal promise
44. assign	___ restore someone's confidence, encourage
45. verdict	___ protect
46. violence	___ ashamed
47. noisy	___ you are close enough to hear what is said
48. crowded	___ goods, products that are sold
49. speak softly	___ when there are very many people in one place
50. privacy	___ put at an angle
51. salvation	___ full of purpose, firmness to do something
52. grace	___ many people together
53. compassion	___ the person who is guilty of having done something
54. shield	___ speak briefly about
55. rejoice	___ look quickly or secretly
56. puzzle	___ be worthy of
57. wrench	___ make more narrow or firm
58. fool	

Questions Section 4   (pages 100-148)

1. How do Briggs and O'Brien try to discredit Osvaldo?

_____

_____

_____

_____

2. How does Steve react to his father's crying?

_____

_____

_____

3. What does this reaction show about Steve?

_____

_____

_____

_____

_____

_____

4. How does Steve react to the news reports about the robbery in the flashbacks? What does this
    tell us about him?

_____

_____

_____

_____

_____

5. What do we learn Steve was doing while Mr. Nesbitt lay dying in his store?

_____

_____

6. On page 119 we are presented with the image of a basketball that lies in the gutter. What does this image suggest or symbolize? (many things!)

_____

_____

_____

_____

_____

_____

_____

_____

7. Why does Steve have a panic attack (he can't breathe) while mopping the floor?

_____

_____

_____

_____

_____

_____

_____

_____

8. Why do you think Steve presents witnesses in montage shots?

_____

_____

_____

_____

_____

9. What do we learn from the reactions shown by the defendants?

_____

_____

_____

10. What's the difference between "I'm not guilty" and "I didn't do it" (138) ?

_____

_____

_____

11. What do we learn about what Steve did on page 140 ?

_____

_____

_____

_____

12. Steve says that the trial isn't about race (146). Do you agree or disagree?

_____

_____

_____

_____

_____

13. What is Ernie's story? Why do you think we are told his story?

_____

_____

_____

_____

_____

_____

14. What does Steve realize after his mother's first visit?

_____

_____

_____

15. Analyze the passages below. Who speaks them? What is striking about them? What is suggested or meant by them? Why are they included at this point in the work, what is their purpose? How might the passages connect to the entire work? Do you agree with the statements made in the passages?

    a. There's so much garbage going through that courtroom, she thinks that anybody in there is going to have a stink on him. (110)

    b. I thought about writing about what happened in the drugstore, but I'd rather not have it in my mind. The pictures of Mr. Nesbitt scare me. (128)

    c. I remember Miss O'Brien saying that it was her job to make me different in the eyes of the jury, different from Bobo and Osvaldo and King. It was me, I thought as I tried not to throw up, that had wanted to be tough like them. (130)

    d. What did I do? I walked into a drugstore to look for some mints, and then I walked out. What was wrong with that? I didn't kill Mr. Nesbitt. Sunset said he committed the crime. Isn't that what being guilty is all about? You actually do something? (140)

    e. Maybe I wouldn't live that long. Maybe I would think about killing myself so I wouldn't have to live that long in here. (144)

    f. She brought me a Bible. The guards had searched it. I wanted to ask if they had found anything in it. Salvation. Grace, maybe. Compassion. She had marked off a passage for me and asked me to read it out loud: "The Lord is my strength and my shield; my heart trusted in him, and I am helped: therefore my heart greatly rejoiceth, and with my song will I praise him". (146)

_____

_____

_____

_____

_____

_____

_____

_____

_____

_____

_____

_____

_____

_____

Writing Tasks

Write at least 200 words.

1. What is manly, what is womanly behavior? (What makes a man "a man", and a woman "a woman"? Are there any differences at all? Should there be?

2. In life, it is good and bad to be different from others. Discuss the (dis)advantages of being like others, and the (dis)advantages of being different.

3. Discrimination is based on assuming that people are different from oneself, and because of such differences "worse" than oneself. Discrimination happens every day. Consider how you might be discriminated against, and how you discriminate against others every day, and what you could do about that.

4. Write a poem (30 lines or more) about the image of the basketball lying in the gutter. (for example: imagine you are the basketball lying in the gutter, and write the poem from his perspective: about Steve, about what you see in the street, about how you feel, etc.)

_____

_____

_____

_____

_____

_____

_____

_____

_____

_____

_____

_____

_____

_____

_____

_____

_____

_____

Vocabulary Section 5   (pages 149-205)

All of the words below are from this reading section. They are listed in order of their appearance in the text. Verbs are given in the infinitive. Match the words with the correct definition by writing the correct number on the line.

1. exterior	___ blame
2. bleary	___ give evidence or a statement in court as a witness
3. liable	___ a series of actions, a lawsuit
4. dis	___ have confidence in, depend on
5. surface	___ tattle, give up a secret that hurts or discredits someone else, snitch
6. mourn	___ make or cause folds in fabrics or skin
7. respective	___ punishment
8. proceed	___ the outside of something
9. proceedings	___ inferior, weaker, lighter, smaller
10. avoid	___ bargain one's way out of full responsibility, confess in exchange for a lighter sentence or no punishment
11. incident	___ happen
12. occur	___ grieve, feel sorrow about a dead person or loss
13. engage	___ release of a prisoner before serving to the end of their sentence on condition of good behavior
14. collar	___ a thing used to sit on
15. refer	___ change to adapt to new conditions, fix, straighten
16. occasion	___ confession, disclosure
17. testify	___ dull, unfocussed (eyes)
18. wrinkle	___ a special event or suitable opportunity
19. sidebar	___ crazy person
20. prejudice	___ disrespect, upset, offend, insult
21. basket case	___ an event causing trouble or problems
22. seat	___ preconceived, irrational, hostile opinion that results in injustice
23. drop a dime	___ uppermost or top layer of something
24. cop a plea	___ continue
25. lesser	___ occupy, involve
26. admission	___ when a judge speaks to the attorneys in court without anyone else hearing what is said
27. penalty	___ held responsible by law
28. parole	___ keep away from, refrain from
29. weight	___ a band around the neck of a piece of clothing or put round a dog's neck
30. rely	___ pass on, transfer, allude to, speak of
31. adjust	___ belonging to each individually, referring to in the order mentioned

Questions Section 5   (pages 149-205)

1. What does the flashback-conversation between Steve and King show?

_____

_____

_____

2. Why, according to Steve, do the inmates fight so much?

_____

_____

3. Why does Steve need his movie more and more?

_____

_____

_____

4. Who is Mrs. Henry and why does she have a problem testifying?

_____

_____

_____

5. What did Mrs. Henry see? How is her testimony discredited? Is Mrs. Henry a good witness?

_____

_____

_____

_____

6. Why does Briggs object to Bobo Evans not wearing a suit?

_____

_____

7. What according to Evans was Steve's role in the robbery?

_____

_____

_____

8. What does Briggs suggest about Evans' testimony on cross?

_____

_____

_____

9. What does O'Brien suggest about Evans' testimony on cross?

_____

_____

_____

10. What did O'Brien ask Steve to write down? Why did she do that? What did he write?

_____

_____

_____

_____

_____

11. What does Steve want to say to his younger brother Jerry? What does he mean by that?

_____

_____

_____

_____

_____

_____

_____

12. Analyze the passages below. Who speaks them? What is striking about them? What is suggested or meant by them? Why are they included at this point in the work, what is their purpose? How might the passages connect to the entire work? Do you agree with the statements made in the passages?

a.   There was a baseball game on but it didn't look real. It was guys in uniforms playing games on a deep green field. They were playing baseball as if baseball was important and as if all the world wasn't in jail, watching them from a completely different world. (155)

b.   In a way I think she was mourning me as if I were dead. (158)

c.   I wouldn't bring anybody into a serious jam unless they wanted to be there. You can't rely on nobody that don't want to be there. (193)

d.   We lie to ourselves here. Maybe we are here because we lie to ourselves. (203)

_____
_____
_____
_____
_____
_____
_____
_____
_____
_____
_____
_____
_____
_____
_____
_____
_____
_____
_____
_____
_____
_____

Writing Tasks

Write at least 200 words.

1. Who do you admire and why? Explain your answer.

2. Write Bobo Evans's or Mrs. Henry's diary entry for the day after his / her testimony.

3. Take Steve's wished advice for his brother Jerry and write of all the tomorrow's of your life.

4. Write a poem (min 30 lines) about the tomorrows of your life or Steve's life.

5. Write the letter Steve might write to Mr. Sawicki.

_____
_____
_____
_____
_____
_____
_____
_____
_____
_____
_____
_____
_____
_____
_____
_____
_____
_____
_____
_____

Vocabulary Section 6   (pages 206-237)

All of the words below are from this reading section. They are listed in order of their appearance in the text. Verbs are given in the infinitive. Match the words with the correct definition by writing the correct number on the line.

1. sincerely	___ show, represent in pictures or words
2. pad	___ spectator, member of an audience, observer
3. wound	___ rely on, be contingent on
4. struggle	___ face up to a problem, meet an enemy
5. access	___ put on clothes
6. fancy	___ forceful, using emotion
7. ability	___ truthful
8. pace	___ decorative, showy, flashy
9. acquaintance	___ to influence or incite to a wrong action
10. tie	___ support, accept, uphold as valid
11. take the stand	___ take back a statement
12. dismiss	___ fight
13. survival	___ guarantee
14. dress	___ a person you know, but not well
15. depend on	___ understanding, merciful, kind
16. occasionally	___ the power or skill to do something
17. confront	___ (verb) walk nervously back and forth
18. solicit	___ (noun) one step, rate or speed of progress
19. withdraw	___ send away, let go, consider unimportant
20. sustain	___ give testimony in court
21. onlooker	___ an injury
22. emphatic	___ a number of sheets of paper glued or otherwise held together at one edge to form a tablet
23. compassionate	___ a way in, the right to see or enter
24. depict	___ genuine, free of deceit or falseness or hypocrisy
25. honest	___ link, connection
26. vouch	___ staying alive
	___ from time to time

Questions Section 6   (pages 206-237)

1. How do Mr. Sawicki's words on page 214 relate to Steve's "movie" ?

_____

_____

_____

_____

_____

_____

2. What "game" do Steve and O'Brien play with the cup? Why do you think she does this?

_____

_____

_____

_____

_____

_____

_____

_____

_____

3. How does Mr. Sawicki describe Steve? Which words probably have the most positive influence on the jury? Why?

_____

_____

_____

_____

4. Do you think Mr. Sawicki is right in his assessment of Steve's personality? How would you describe Steve? Justify your answer with references to the text.

_____

_____

_____

_____

5. Analyze the passages below. Who speaks them? What is striking about them? What is suggested or meant by them? Why are they included at this point in the work, what is their purpose? How might the passages connect to the entire work? Do you agree with the statements made in the passages?

   a. The prosecutor said I was lying. I wanted to ask her what she expected me to do when telling the truth was going to get me 10 years. (220)

   b. Only truth I know is I don't want to be in here with you ugly dudes. (221)

   c. Truth is something you gave up when you were out there on the street. Now you talking survival. (222)

_____

_____

_____

_____

_____

_____

_____

_____

_____

_____

_____

_____

_____

_____

_____

_____

_____

_____

_____

_____

_____

_____

Writing Tasks

Write at least 150 words.

1. Write the cup-conversation-training Steve and O'Brien have.

2. If you were the judge, which sentences would you give King and Steve respectively? Justify your answer.

3. Write the closing argument Petrocelli, O'Brien, or Briggs might give. (Choose this task only if you have not yet finished reading the book.)

_____

_____

_____

_____

_____

_____

_____

_____

_____

_____

_____

_____

_____

_____

_____

_____

_____

_____

_____

_____

_____

_____

_____

_____

Vocabulary Section 7   (pages 238-281)

All of the words below are from this reading section. They are listed in order of their appearance in the text. Verbs are given in the infinitive. Match the words with the correct definition by writing the correct number on the line.

1. accusation	___ a person frequently in the company of another, mate, pal
2. demonstrate	___ uncomfortable, awkward, unsure, apprehensive
3. offer	___ to take for granted without proof, suppose
4. implicate	___ being observant and thoughtful
5. capable of	___ to confront
6. admit	___ easily deceived or tricked, naïve, believing everything
7. unemployed	___ spoiled, poorly done, messed up
8. underemployed	___ rearrange, revise, correct
9. produce	___ quest, search
10. assume	___ bring back
11. urge	___ legal right of possession
12. pursuer	___ be a sign of, point to
13. decent	___ compared to, in contrast to
14. law-abiding	___ a quantity or degree of something
15. ultimately	___ twist out of shape, deform, misrepresent
16. proof	___ positive achievement
17. reject	___ follower, person who tries to catch someone
18. consign	___ charge of wrongdoing
19. edge	___ a line or border of something
20. patience	___ propose, promise
21. attentiveness	___ being calm in the face of delay, not restless
22. review	___ false show of bravery
23. indicate	___ in identical manner, degree, or extent
24. awesome	___ mirror image
25. ownership	___ opposition, rivalry, dispute, controversy
26. trace	___ only
27. suggest	___ threatening to cause harm or evil
28. elicit	___ give focus to
29. constitute	___ person who shares business affairs of another, ally
30. convince	___ of little depth, superficial
31. shallow	___ propose
32. gullible	___ evidence
33. as opposed to	___ prove the truth of something, confirm
34. hide	___ formally relieve from charge or fault, declare not guilty, discharge
35. face	___ officially hand over, banish to
36. circumstances	___ to push or force along, strongly recommend and move to action
37. reinforce	___ persuade, make worthy of belief
38. acquit	___ to conceal from sight, cover up
39. contention	___ strengthen, support
40. pursuit	___ act of selling something
41. verify	___ specific situation or condition surrounding a person
42. merely	___ refuse to have or accept, cast out
43. sale	___ show (use for 2 words!)
44. uneasy	___ have no job
45. botched	___ inspiring fear or great respect of some power
46. equally	___ form, be part of
47. successful	___ ease, free from
48. relieve	___ draw out, evoke, bring out
49. associate	___ finally
50. companion	___ show involvement, connect to a crime
51. restore	___ critically look at, summarize or examine
52. a measure	___ follow evidence or footprints to find out, discover
53. bravado	___ following and respecting the law
54. menacing	___ have insufficient work
55. edit	___ be competent, be inclined to do something
56. sharpen	___ conforming to standards of propriety, kind, respectable
57. distort	___ to confess
58. reflection	

Questions Section 7   (pages 238-281)

1. In what way are the closing arguments of Briggs, O'Brien, and Petrocelli different? Read closely and evaluate what strategies and arguments they use to reach their goal.

Attorney	Main purpose and focus	Tone, diction, style (e.g. formal, aggressive, polite, colloquial, sophisticated, using a range of registers, etc.)	Relation to audience and use of rhetorical devices (e.g. questions, humor, puns, ridiculing others, use of pronouns, emotional appeals, etc.)
Briggs			
O'Brien			
Petrocelli			

2. Which one do you find most convincing? Why?

_____

_____

_____

_____

_____

3. Who do you think is the best lawyer of the three? Justify your answer.

_____

_____

_____

_____

_____

_____

4. What does Steve mean by "the case fills me" (269) ?

_____

_____

_____

_____

5. What does Steve think about that night while the jury is deliberating?

_____

_____

_____

_____

6. Why is the father distant from Steve after the trial?

_____

_____

_____

7. Is Steve a reliable narrator? Justify your answer with references to the text.

_____

_____

_____

_____

_____

_____

_____

_____

8. Do you think justice was served in this trial? Explain your answer in detail.

_____

_____

_____

_____

_____

_____

_____

_____

_____

_____

_____

_____

_____

_____

_____

_____

_____

_____

9. Analyze the passages below. Who speaks them? What is striking about them? What is suggested or meant by them? Why are they included at this point in the work, what is their purpose? How might the passages connect to the entire work? Do you agree with the statements made in the passages?

    a. What was the decision I made? To walk down the streets? To get up in the morning? To talk to King? What decisions did I make? What decisions didn't I make? But I don't want to think about decisions, just my case. (270)

    b. I keep editing the movies, making the scenes right. Sharpening the dialog. "A getover. I don't do getovers", I say in the movie in my mind, my chin tilted slightly upward. "I know what right is, what truth is. I don't do tightropes, moral or otherwise." I put strings in the background. Cellos. Violas. (271)

_____

_____

_____

_____

_____

_____

_____

_____

_____

_____

_____

_____

_____

_____

_____

_____

_____

_____

_____

_____

_____

_____

Final Writing Tasks

Choose two of the tasks below. Write at least 300 words for each.

1. Write a letter to Steve's mother explaining to her Steve's obsession with his films.

2. Write O'Brien's diary entry on the day of Steve's acquittal. Include whether she thinks justice was served or not and what she thinks about Steve.

3. Write a newspaper article and a newspaper editorial about the trial and its outcome.

4. Would you rather be a prosecutor or a defense attorney? Justify your answer by using examples from this text.

5. How does your being a European woman, man, non-adult, or someone not living in a large city affect your reading of the text?

6. The book won several major writing awards. Why? For what do you think it received these awards? Would you give it an award and for what?

6b. Write the speech that might be given to convince an awards committee to give, or not to give, a prize to Walter Dean Myers.

7. There are several descriptions of very disturbing images in this book, for example of violence, rapes, sexual attack, etc.

    a) Imagine you are the principal of the school. Write a letter to the English teacher giving him / her instructions on how to handle this type of realism in the novel with students in the classroom.

    b) Imagine you are a parent of a student reading this novel. Write a letter to the English teacher explaining why you want or don't want your child to read this book as a class assignment at that grade level.

_____

_____

_____

_____

_____

_____

_____

_____

_____

_____

_____

Analysis

A Fact and Non-Fact

Diagram the murder. Include the details that you learn in the story of what occurred and who was there. Separate known fact from opinion or hearsay in two columns.

Fact	Opinion (non-fact)

B Witness Chart

Summarize the different witness statements in the chart below, and outline their reliability.

Witness Name	Claims	How are the claims questioned by the defense?	Your impression of the witness: reliable or not and why?

C } Guilty or Not Guilty ? Reach a Verdict !

Imagine you are a juror in the trial of Steve Harmon and James King. On the legal pads below, take notes based only on what you know from trial (not from Steve's journal). At the bottom of the page write your preferred verdict and justify it in 2-3 sentences.

THE STATE OF NEW YORK VS. STEVE HARMON

What suggests the defendant's guilt:

What constitutes reasonable doubt:

JUROR NUMBER : ____

VERDICT : _____

JUSTIFICATION:

C 2 Guilty or Not Guilty ? Reach a Verdict !

Imagine you are a juror in the trial of Steve Harmon and James King. On the legal pads below, take notes based only on what you know from trial (not from Steve's journal). At the bottom of the page write your preferred verdict and justify it in 2-3 sentences.

THE STATE OF NEW YORK VS. JAMES KING

What suggests the defendant's guilt:	What constitutes reasonable doubt:

JUROR NUMBER : ____   VERDICT : _____

JUSTIFICATION:

C 3 Guilty or Not Guilty ? Reach a Verdict !

Imagine you are a juror in the trial of Steve Harmon. You have been given access to and have read Steve's journal. Take notes on the legal pad below to determine your verdict. Is it different from C1? Why?

THE STATE OF NEW YORK VS. STEVE HARMON

What suggests the defendant's guilt:

What constitutes reasonable doubt:

JUROR NUMBER : ____   VERDICT : _____

JUSTIFICATION:

C 4 Reach a Verdict ! Jury Deliberation Role Play

Using your legal pads notes, prepare and stage a role play of the jury's deliberation. Assign roles and tasks to organize the deliberation. For example: who's the foreman, who will keep a discussion log, who will be the timekeeper, who will intervene if a discussion gets out of hand, what props will you need and for what, will you try to have an even distribution of juror's with guilty / non-guilty verdicts at the outset of the role play or make it luck of the draw, will you include an even number of male, female, black, white, ethnic jurors, will you include a pre-activity showing the voire dire (jury selection process), etc..

Decide in advance whether Steve's journal is admissible and shall be included or not, whether a unanimous verdict is required, whether and what kind of a majority decision suffices, and under which circumstances you can declare yourself a hung jury.

Space for notes to prepare your jury deliberation role play:

Questions for further consideration and discussion and more ideas for writing tasks and role play activities

1. From the beginning, Steve likens his "movie" to *Star Wars*. What does this link suggest? Which *Star-Wars*-like qualities does Steve's movie have? Justify your answer.

2. Do you think the jury system is a good system? Explain your answer.

3. Is Steve a monster? What are qualities of a (human) monster?

4. How does the narrative technique influence your view of the other participants in the crime?

5. Consider the role race plays in the text. For example, does it matter what the race of the judge, attorneys, witnesses, and defendant is? What about Mr. Nesbitt's race? Would the story change if Steve were white? How?

6. Consider the role social status and class plays in the text. Would the story be different if Steve's parents were rich? How?

7. Why does the narrator include discussions of some bodily functions quite frequently? Identify references to bodily functions and discuss their possible significance.

8. Is the screenplay / journal format an effective way of telling the story? When is the form most effective, when the least effective and why? Return to the advice Mr. Sawicki gives on pages 19 and 214. Do you think Steve achieves this in his screenplay? Use examples from the text to support your answer.

9. Why does the justice system use the terms "guilty" and "not guilty", instead of "guilty" and "innocent"? What is the difference between "not guilty" and "innocent" ? How would a justice system based on the idea of "guilty until proven innocent" be different?

10. Are fact and non-fact the same as truth and non-truth? How might characters in the novel answer this question? Choose a character and write an answer from his /her perspective.

11. Write the newspaper article reporting Mr. Nesbitt's death and the subsequent arrests.

12. Imagine Steve and Mr. Nesbitt could meet or speak. Write or stage their conversation in a role play.

13. Prepare and stage a talk-show in which a host presents all or some of these guests: Steve, Steve's parents, Steve's brother Jerry, Mr. Briggs, a policeman or detective who worked the case, one or more members of Mr. Nesbitt's family, Mr. Sawicki, Osvaldo's ex-girlfriend, a neutral legal expert.

14. Create a film following only Steve's screenplay instructions.

15. Create a film including Steve's screenplay and his journal.

Text Type Composition Strategies

How to Write a Formal Letter

When writing a formal letter you must follow specific formatting, punctuation, and wording requirements. Read the information below to learn more about writing this text type.

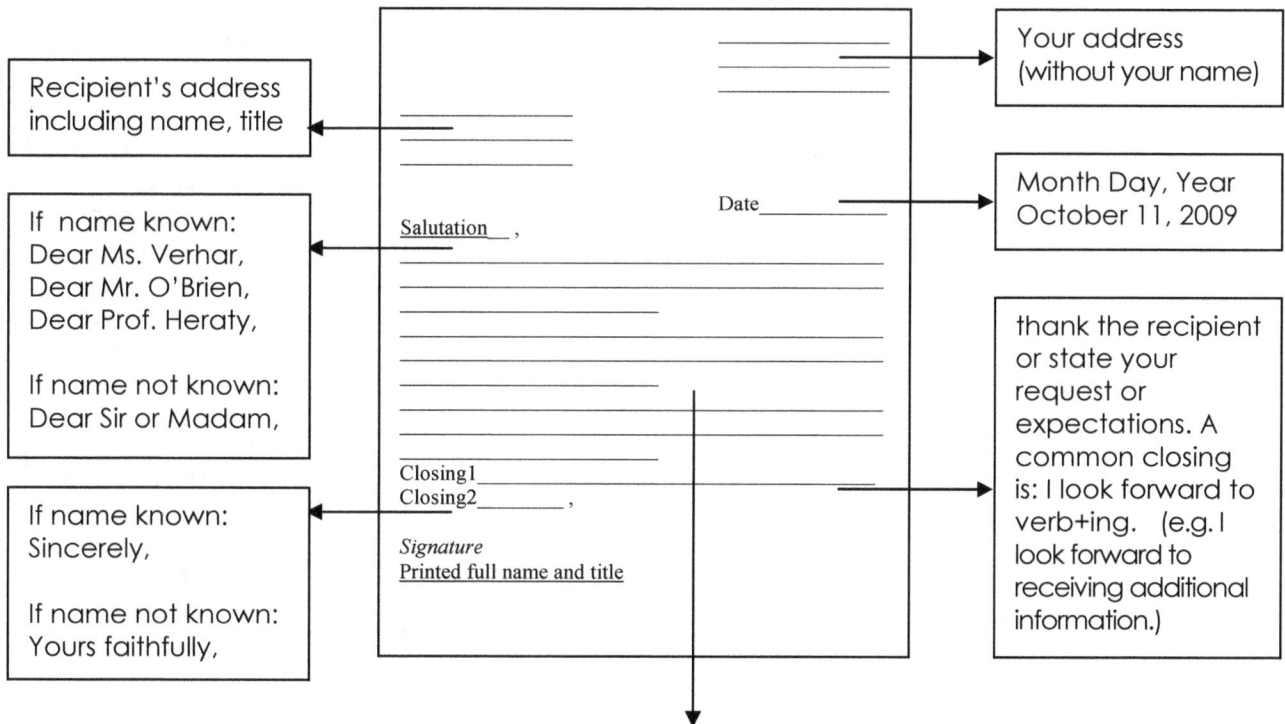

Recipient's address including name, title

If name known:
Dear Ms. Verhar,
Dear Mr. O'Brien,
Dear Prof. Heraty,

If name not known:
Dear Sir or Madam,

If name known:
Sincerely,

If name not known:
Yours faithfully,

Salutation   ,

Date_____

Closing1_____
Closing2_____ ,

Signature
Printed full name and title

Your address (without your name)

Month Day, Year
October 11, 2009

thank the recipient or state your request or expectations. A common closing is: I look forward to verb+ing. (e.g. I look forward to receiving additional information.)

In the first lines of your letter, clearly state your intention or purpose for writing. Always be polite (even in a letter of complaint!), use complete sentences with correct punctuation, structure your letter in paragraphs, try to use formal vocabulary, do not use short verb forms (can't = cannot, don't = do not, he's = he is, aren't = are not, etc.) and do not use exclamation marks (!).

How to Write an Informal Letter

When writing an informal letter you are freer than when writing a formal one, but you must still follow certain rules. Keep in mind that informal letters can range from very informal to semi-formal. An informal letter that you write to a very close friend who is the same age as you will use different wording and structure than an informal letter you write to your grandmother thanking her for a birthday present, or an informal letter you write to a colleague or superior. Read the information below to learn more about writing this text type.

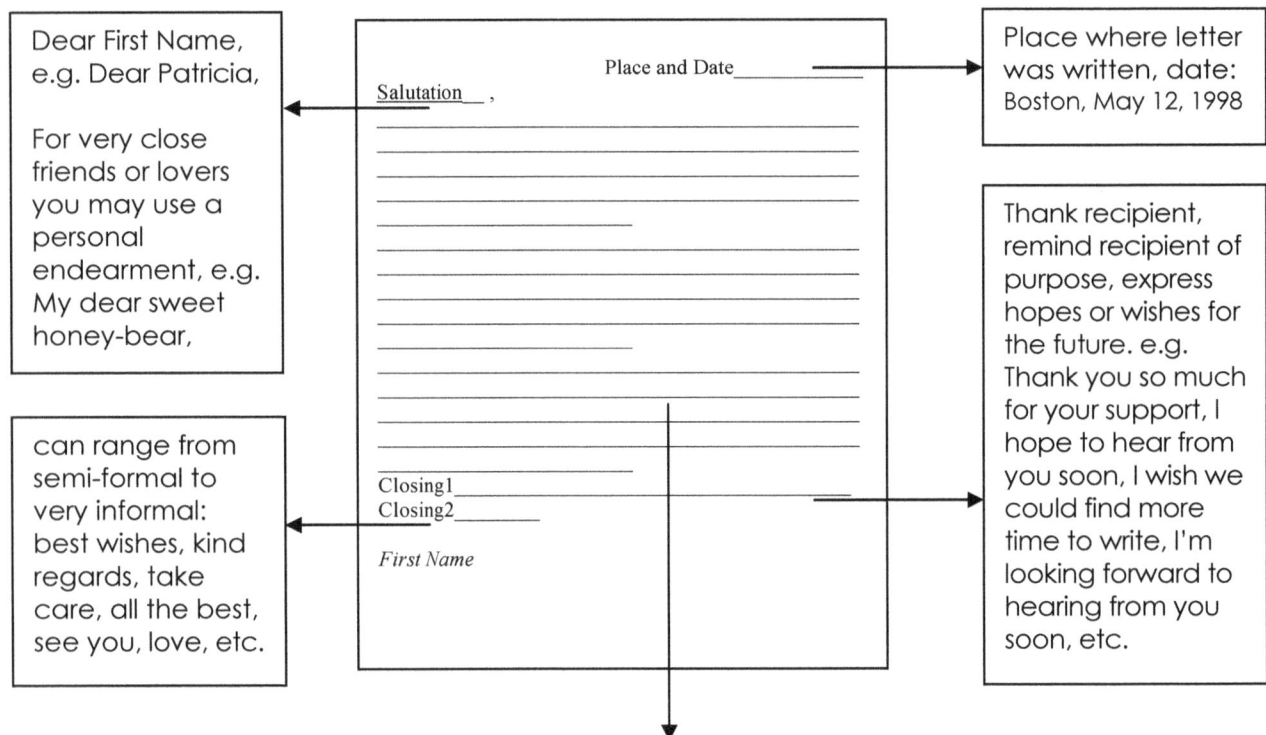

Dear First Name, e.g. Dear Patricia,

For very close friends or lovers you may use a personal endearment, e.g. My dear sweet honey-bear,

can range from semi-formal to very informal: best wishes, kind regards, take care, all the best, see you, love, etc.

Place and Date_____

Salutation___ ,

Closing1_____
Closing2_____

First Name

Place where letter was written, date: Boston, May 12, 1998

Thank recipient, remind recipient of purpose, express hopes or wishes for the future. e.g. Thank you so much for your support, I hope to hear from you soon, I wish we could find more time to write, I'm looking forward to hearing from you soon, etc.

Depending on how well you know the recipient and how informal your letter is, you may use very informal expressions, short verb forms, abbreviations, colloquialisms, make references to mutual knowledge, shared experiences, express opinions about friends, colleagues, events, be personal and show emotion (enthusiasm, anger, sadness, etc.). Your letter to a close friend need not be structured in paragraphs, but it makes it easier to read. Writing to a very close friend also allows you to use stream-of-consciousness technqiue in which you just write whatever pops into your head and jump from one topic to another. You may further ask for feedback with expressions such as "right?", "don't you agree?", or "what do you think?", and use exclamation marks for effect. A semi-formal letter on the other hand will try to keep emotions, colloquialisms and abbreviations to a minimum (unless they are work-related argot), and use paragraph structure and more formal phrases, salutations, closings, and should be signed with your first and last name.

How to Write a Diary Entry

Read the information below to learn more about writing this text type.

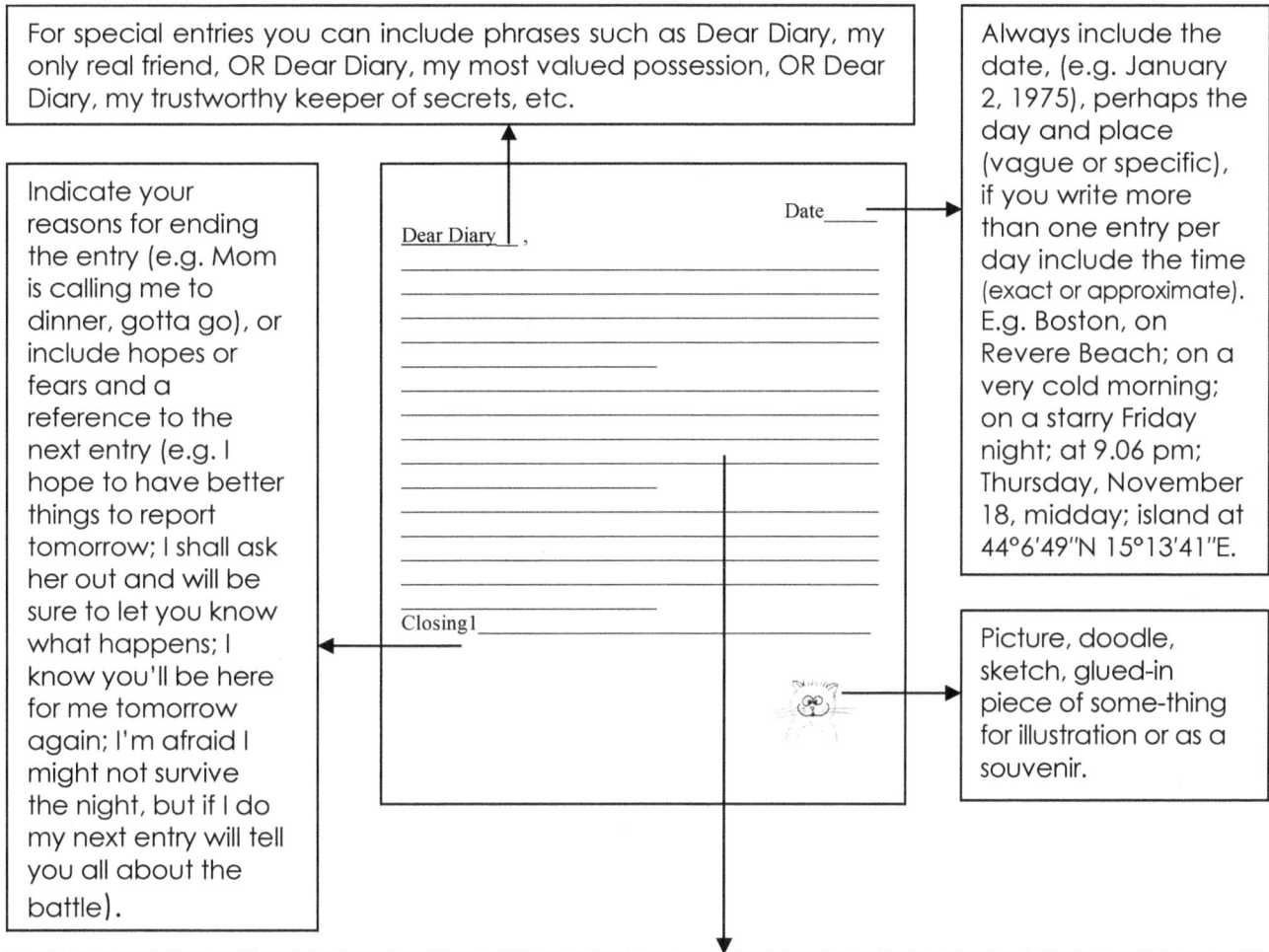

For special entries you can include phrases such as Dear Diary, my only real friend, OR Dear Diary, my most valued possession, OR Dear Diary, my trustworthy keeper of secrets, etc.

Always include the date, (e.g. January 2, 1975), perhaps the day and place (vague or specific), if you write more than one entry per day include the time (exact or approximate). E.g. Boston, on Revere Beach; on a very cold morning; on a starry Friday night; at 9.06 pm; Thursday, November 18, midday; island at 44°6′49″N 15°13′41″E.

Indicate your reasons for ending the entry (e.g. Mom is calling me to dinner, gotta go), or include hopes or fears and a reference to the next entry (e.g. I hope to have better things to report tomorrow; I shall ask her out and will be sure to let you know what happens; I know you'll be here for me tomorrow again; I'm afraid I might not survive the night, but if I do my next entry will tell you all about the battle).

Dear Diary ,

Date_____

Closing1_____

Picture, doodle, sketch, glued-in piece of some-thing for illustration or as a souvenir.

In many ways writing a diary entry is like writing a letter or speaking to a very close friend. Diary entries can range from very informal to very formal – particularly if they are intended as evidence of a scientific experiment or expedition. If you expect only yourself to be the audience of your diary text, you may use very informal expressions, short verb forms, abbreviations, colloquialisms, make references to mutual knowledge, previously reported experiences, express opinions that you would not dare utter elsewhere than in the secrecy of your diary. Be opinionated, emotional, desperate, judgmental, seething, whatever fits! Your diary entry should be personal and emphasize your personal thoughts and feelings. Show emotions (enthusiasm, anger, sadness, etc.) in your style and choice of words. Use exclamation marks, punctuation, play with different font sizes and shapes to underscore your words and emotions, you may even include doodles and symbols. You will always address your diary directly, not only in the initial phrase, but also throughout the entry (e.g. I am telling this to you, my only friend, to show you...). Treat the diary as if it were a real person with a personality you can comment on and refer to. You can also use a range of registers playfully in your diary entry, perhaps assuming different personas and voices (and usually exaggerating these to make your point). Use humor, wit, sarcasm, make cynical remarks if it fits the topic and the person writing. An informal diary entry need not be structured in paragraphs, but it makes it easier to read. It also allows you to use stream-of-consciousness technique in which you just write whatever pops into your head and jump from one topic to another. You may further ask for feedback with expressions such as "right?", "don't you agree?", or "what do you think?", and you may answer your own questions. All diary entries, whether formal or informal, should include much detail (who, what, where, when, why, how), and include reasons for writing as well as ending the diary entry at a specific point in time.

How to Write a Newspaper Article

Read the information below to learn more about writing this text type.

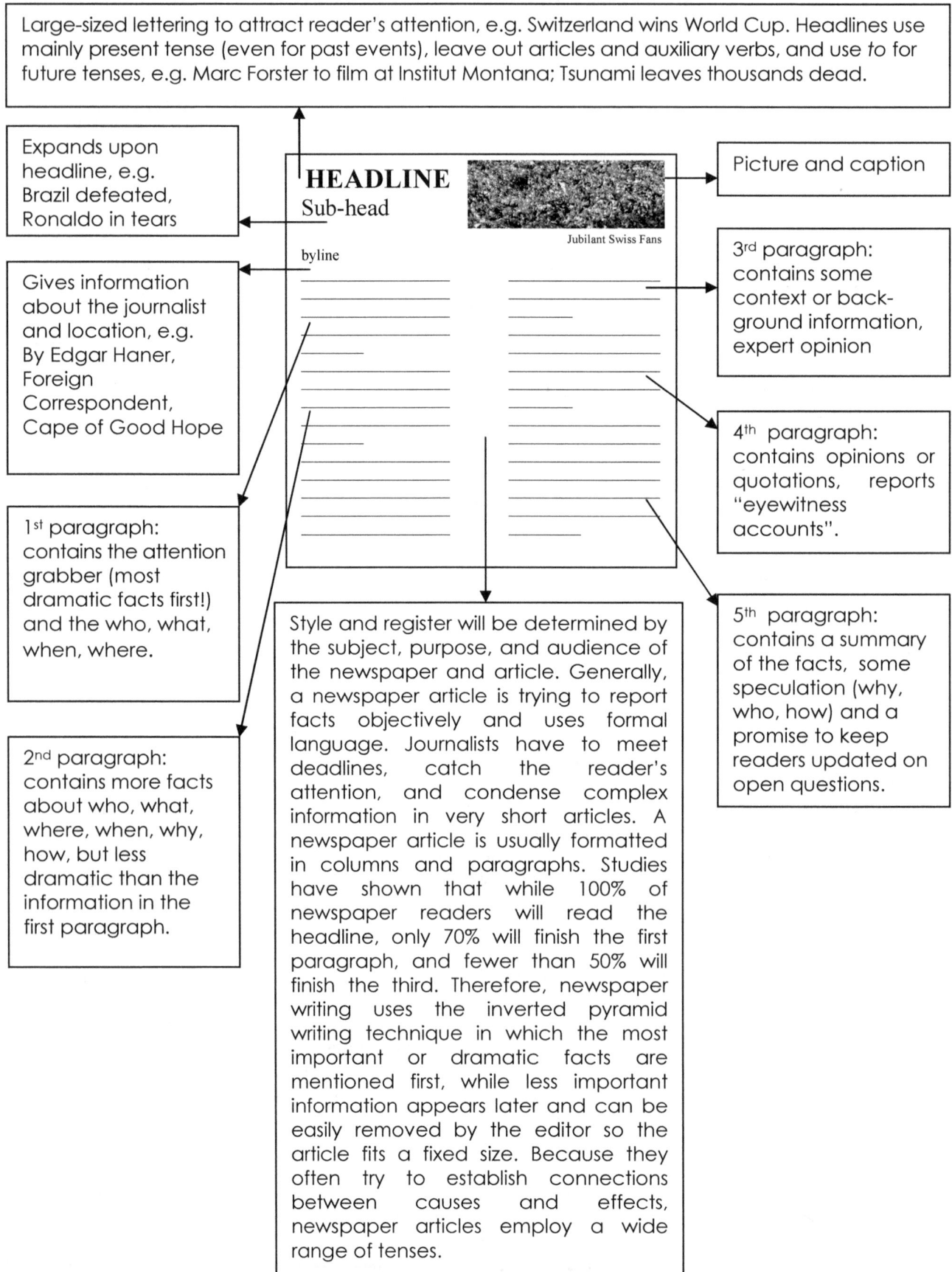

Large-sized lettering to attract reader's attention, e.g. Switzerland wins World Cup. Headlines use mainly present tense (even for past events), leave out articles and auxiliary verbs, and use *to* for future tenses, e.g. Marc Forster to film at Institut Montana; Tsunami leaves thousands dead.

Expands upon headline, e.g. Brazil defeated, Ronaldo in tears

Gives information about the journalist and location, e.g. By Edgar Haner, Foreign Correspondent, Cape of Good Hope

1st paragraph: contains the attention grabber (most dramatic facts first!) and the who, what, when, where.

2nd paragraph: contains more facts about who, what, where, when, why, how, but less dramatic than the information in the first paragraph.

HEADLINE
Sub-head

byline

Jubilant Swiss Fans

Picture and caption

3rd paragraph: contains some context or back-ground information, expert opinion

4th paragraph: contains opinions or quotations, reports "eyewitness accounts".

5th paragraph: contains a summary of the facts, some speculation (why, who, how) and a promise to keep readers updated on open questions.

Style and register will be determined by the subject, purpose, and audience of the newspaper and article. Generally, a newspaper article is trying to report facts objectively and uses formal language. Journalists have to meet deadlines, catch the reader's attention, and condense complex information in very short articles. A newspaper article is usually formatted in columns and paragraphs. Studies have shown that while 100% of newspaper readers will read the headline, only 70% will finish the first paragraph, and fewer than 50% will finish the third. Therefore, newspaper writing uses the inverted pyramid writing technique in which the most important or dramatic facts are mentioned first, while less important information appears later and can be easily removed by the editor so the article fits a fixed size. Because they often try to establish connections between causes and effects, newspaper articles employ a wide range of tenses.

Final Factsheet

Keyword-question	Answer / Explanation / Justification
Author	
Place and date of first publication	
Narrator	
Point-of-view	
Genre(s)	
Setting	
Protagonist	
Antagonist(s)	
Foils	
3 main conflicts	

5 adjectives that best describe this work for you	
Purpose or message of book	
Most memorable	
What you liked best	
What you liked the least	
What you have learned	

www.ingramcontent.com/pod-product-compliance
Lightning Source LLC
Chambersburg PA
CBHW080857090426

42736CB00016B/3211